NORRIE EXPLORES...

NEW YORK CITY

Help Norrie to solve the clues on a fascinating adventure!

World Book, Inc.
180 North LaSalle Street
Suite 900
Chicago, Illinois 60601
USA

For information about other World Book publications, visit our website at www.worldbook.com or call 1-800-WORLDBK (967-5325). For information about sales to schools and libraries, call 1-800-975-3250 (United States), or 1-800-837-5365 (Canada).

Library of Congress Cataloging-in-Publication Data for this volume has been applied for.

Norrie Explores ...
ISBN: 978-0-7166-5303-5 (set, hc.)

Norrie Explores ... New York
ISBN: 978-0-7166-5309-7 (hc.)
ISBN: 978-0-7166-5329-5 (pf.)

Also available as:
ISBN: 978-0-7166-5319-6 (e-book)

Staff

Executive Committee
President: Geoff Broderick
Vice President, Editorial: Tom Evans
Vice President, Finance: Donald D. Keller
Vice President, International: Eddy Kisman
Vice President, Technology: Jason Dole
Director, Human Resources: Bev Ecker

Editorial
Senior Editor/Indexer: Shawn Brennan
Editor/Researcher: Lynn Durbin
Content Creator: Jenna Neely
Curriculum Designer: Caroline Davidson
Project Coordinator: Kaile Kilner
Proofreader: Nathalie Strassheim

Graphics and Design
Senior Visual Communications Designer: Melanie Bender
Senior Media Editor: Rosalia Bledsoe

Acknowledgments

Writer: Madeline King
Illustrator: Mike Garton, The Bright Agency
Designer: Francis Lea

Cover: Norrie artwork by Mike Garton, The Bright Agency; © Mihai Simonia, Shutterstock

4-9 © Shutterstock
10-11 Joe Shlabotnik (licensed under CC BY-NC-SA 2.0); © Citizen of the Planet/Alamy Images; © James Andrews, Shutterstock
12-13 © Shutterstock
14-15 © travelwild/Shutterstock; Library of Congress; © Michele Vacchiano, Shutterstock
16-17 © Shutterstock
18-19 © nyker/Shutterstock; © Hemis/Alamy Images; © Sean Pavone, Shutterstock
20-21 © Andrey Bayda, Shutterstock; Richard Termine. This is from the 2021 production of *Jim Henson's Emmet Otter's Jug-Band Christmas;* © David Pereiras, Shutterstock; © singh_lens/Shutterstock
22-29 © Shutterstock
30-31 © You production/Shutterstock; © Agnieszka Gaul, Shutterstock; Sphilbrick (CC BY-SA 3.0)
32-39 © Shutterstock
40-41 © dibrova/Shutterstock; © Patti McConville, Alamy Images; © a katz/Shutterstock
42-43 © Shutterstock
46-47 © Shutterstock; MusikAnimal (CC BY-SA 4.0); © Citizen of the Planet/Alamy Images; © Michael Ventura, Alamy Images
48-49 © Shutterstock; © Richard Green, Alamy Images; © Anastassiyatsvey/Dreamstime
50-51 © Shutterstock

Contents

Welcome to New York City! 4
Islands 6
Boroughs and Neighborhoods 8
The Bronx, Queens, and Staten Island 10
Manhattan 12
Harlem 14
Central Park 16
American Museum of Natural History 18
Times Square 20
Grand Central Terminal 22
Sports 24
Empire State Building 26
Uptown and Downtown Parks 28
Greenwich Village 30
The Financial District 32
One World Trade Center 34
Ellis Island 36
Liberty Island 38
Brooklyn 40
Coney Island 42
New York City Map 44
A Day in New York City 46
Where Am I? 48
Photos from New York City 50
Engage Your Reader 52
Extend Through Writing 54
Answers 55
Glossary and Index 56

Welcome to New York City!

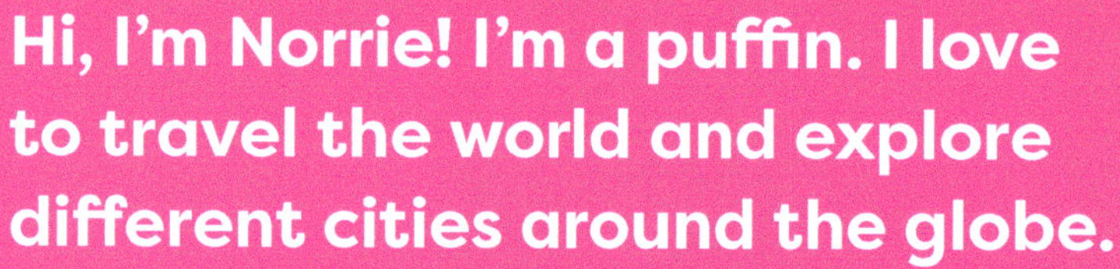

Hi, I'm Norrie! I'm a puffin. I love to travel the world and explore different cities around the globe.

Today, I'm in New York City, the largest city in the United States and one of the largest in the world. Because of its importance as a cultural and entertainment center, New York City is also called the "Big Apple."

Why am I visiting New York City today? The city is home to many pigeons, and I am here to visit some of my pigeon friends! They want to meet at the amusement park in Coney Island. Coney Island is a famous entertainment area in Brooklyn, a section of New York City.

There are roller coasters, beaches, and food. And, like humans, we birds enjoy these pleasures!

My friends have given me clues to solve. They know I love a puzzle! The clues will be photos, words, or objects. Each clue will lead me to the next place to visit. As I follow the clues, I will make my way to Coney Island. This hunt is a great way to visit New York City. Let's get started!

Islands

I am excited to show you around New York City! Let's begin with an important fact about New York. It is mostly a city of islands. That was what our word scramble spelled. Each island has its own story.

The earliest people known to have lived in the New York City area were Indigenous (native) people who spoke an Algonquian language. Several related tribes lived peacefully on the shores of New York Harbor and along the banks of the Hudson and East rivers.

Settlers from Europe arrived in the early 1600's. They bought this little sliver of land from the Native Americans who lived and hunted there. Legend tells us that the Europeans traded cloth and other trinkets worth about 24 dollars for the land. But the truth is probably a lot more complicated.

Soon, Europeans were settling on nearby Long Island, too. The Long Island settlements closest to Manhattan developed strong ties with Manhattan.

Ellis Island was where many immigrants officially entered the United States.

Staten Island was mostly small farms until about 50 years ago. Then the Verrazano-Narrows Bridge was built in the 1960's. More people moved to the island. But even today, it isn't as crowded as Manhattan and the rest of New York City.

Liberty Island is home to the Statue of Liberty.

Boroughs and Neighborhoods

Let's take a look at how New York City is organized.

New York City is made up of five main sections. Each section is called a borough (BUR oh). Remember when I said that most of New York City lies on islands? All but one of the boroughs are located on islands. The boroughs are divided into neighborhoods – more than 250 altogether. Immigrants from the same country often settled, and still settle, in the same neighborhood. They brought with them their language and customs, giving many neighborhoods an international flavor.

BRONX

MANHATTAN

QUEENS

BROOKLYN

STATEN ISLAND

You can get to almost every borough by using the subway system. And our clue was a card we can use to ride the subway! Subways in New York even go under the East and Harlem rivers. To get to Staten Island, though, we have to ride the ferry. New York City's subway system, one of the largest in the world, provides passenger service on about 660 miles (1,060 kilometers) of track.

The Bronx, Queens, and Staten Island

Now we will learn about the Bronx, Queens, and Staten Island.

The Bronx: I like a good zoo, and each of these boroughs has one. But only the Bronx Zoo has a bug carousel. There is a long-legged praying mantis and a grasshopper. Well, that explains the picture. You can even ride a dung beetle! In cool weather, the carousel closes its sliding glass door to keep us warm.

Queens: At the New York Hall of Science, we can plunge our wings into activities and help out in science demonstrations. The borough of Queens has several well-known sections, most of them residential.

Staten Island: Remember, we'll have to take a ferry to get to Staten Island. That's okay with me. I love riding the Staten Island Ferry! At Historic Richmond Town, let's find out what life was like for kids and their families during the 1600's, 1700's, and 1800's. We'll tour such buildings as a tinsmith's shop and a basket maker's house and explore a working farm.

Astoria, in northwestern Queens, is home to many people of Greek ancestry and descendants of other immigrant groups. And many people from Latin America and South Asia have settled in historic Jackson Heights.

Basket maker's house, Historic Richmond Town

This sleep mask suggests that the next spot will be nap-related. Good, because touring is exhausting.

Manhattan

There's a song about New York City that calls it the "city that never sleeps." In the borough of Manhattan, that may actually be true. I think that's why we were given a sleep mask – to show that we'll never need it!

There's always something to do, day or night. Even the subway runs 24 hours a day! Manhattan has the tallest buildings in New York City. It also has some of the most important schools and colleges in the United States. And it has the most famous theater district in the world. One of my favorite things to do here is to take a boat tour all the way around Manhattan Island. From the deck of a boat, the buildings look like mountains. Later, when we are in the streets of Manhattan, it will feel like we're walking in a canyon.

Manhattan is surrounded by the Hudson River to the west, Upper New York Bay to the south, the East River to the east, and the Harlem River to the north and northeast.

Harlem

Let's take the subway to Uptown Manhattan, to 125th Street. We'll be in Harlem.

We could spend days here in the center of Black culture. The neighborhood stretches almost from the Hudson River to the East River on the northern part of Manhattan Island.

Of all the museums, theaters, and restaurants, we should visit the Apollo Theater. It's been around for more than 100 years. Many great entertainers have performed here – that's why our microphone led us here!

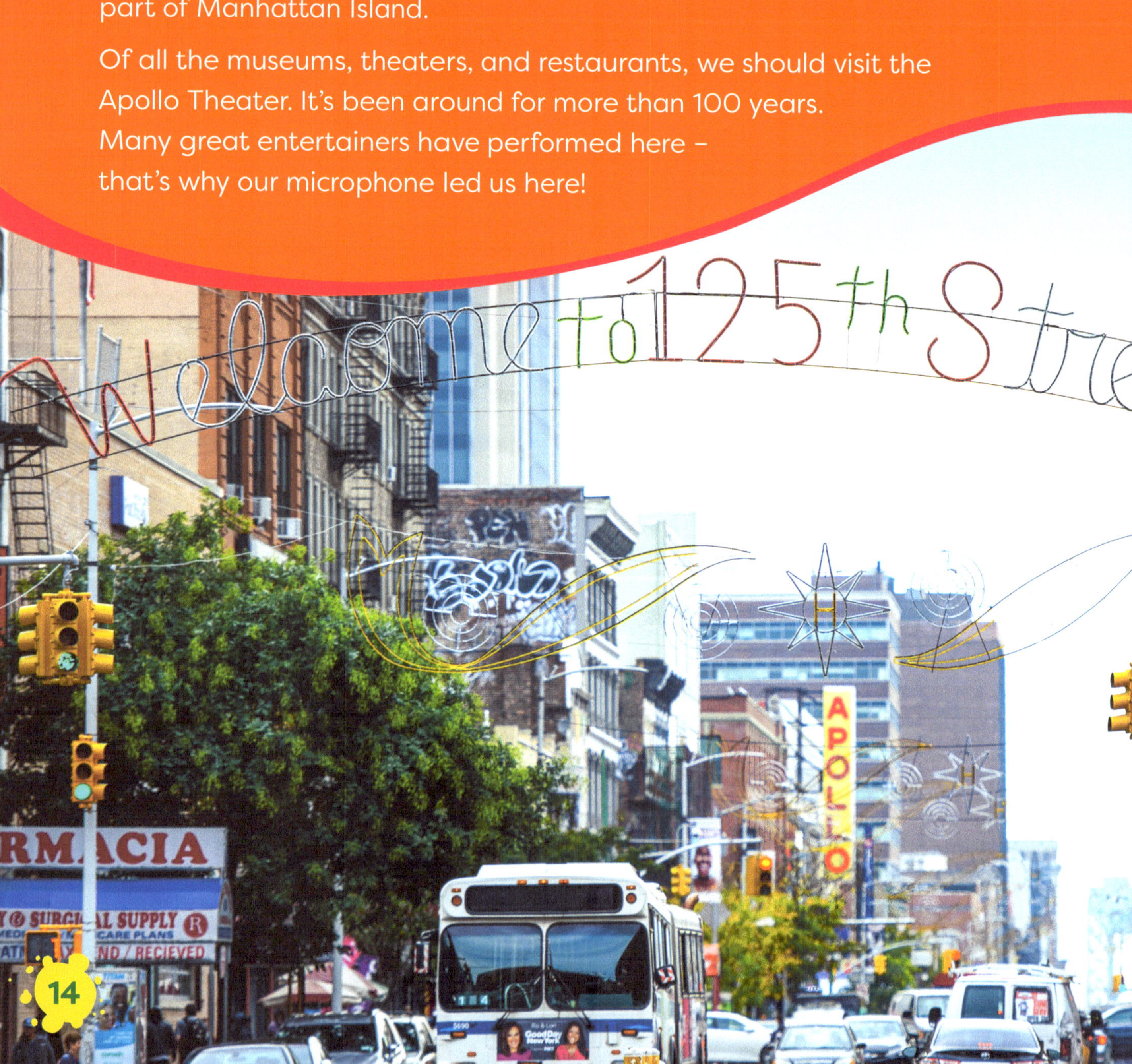

The Harlem Renaissance was an important movement in Black literature and other arts during the 1920's and early 1930's. The artistic "renaissance," which means rebirth, was set in Harlem, because it was the center of Black cultural life during that period. During the Harlem Renaissance, writers and artists explored the excellence of Black life.

Major African American writers during the Harlem Renaissance included Arna Bontemps, Countee Cullen, Langston Hughes (shown here), Zora Neale Hurston, James Weldon Johnson, Claude McKay, and Jean Toomer.

Are you hungry yet? I am. Harlem is packed with different kinds of food. American hamburgers or crab cakes? Southern catfish? Cajun? French? Italian? You pick!

Central Park

How about a stroll through Central Park? It is hard to miss Central Park. It covers 50 city blocks – and it's green!

Central Park covers 843 acres (341 hectares). It runs from 59th to 110th streets between Fifth Avenue and Central Park West. It separates Manhattan's Upper East Side and Upper West Side. The park is bounded by Midtown to the south and Harlem to the north. Bring a blanket if you want to rest a while!

Did you know we can take a boat out on Central Park Lake? Or we could cross Bow Bridge and go hiking in the Ramble. The Ramble is a little forest – right in the middle of the big city! We can sit down on our blanket here.

At the southern part of the park, there is an entrance to the Central Park Zoo, New York City's first zoo. Let's make sure to explore the Tisch Children's Zoo, tucked into the northeast corner of the bigger zoo.

American Museum of Natural History

New York is crammed with museums. Let's go to one about life on Earth!

The American Museum of Natural History has its own subway stop. You step out into the Upper West Side neighborhood, across the street from Central Park. Inside, I like to go straight to the dinosaur wing. My favorites are *Tyrannosaurus rex* and *Triceratops.* You can choose your favorite from about 100 dinosaur skeletons. I wonder which dinosaur is missing this tooth. If you visit December through May, head to the second floor and the Butterfly Conservatory. It's warm inside the vivarium, an indoor enclosure for living plants and animals, and you get to hang out with hundreds of butterflies.

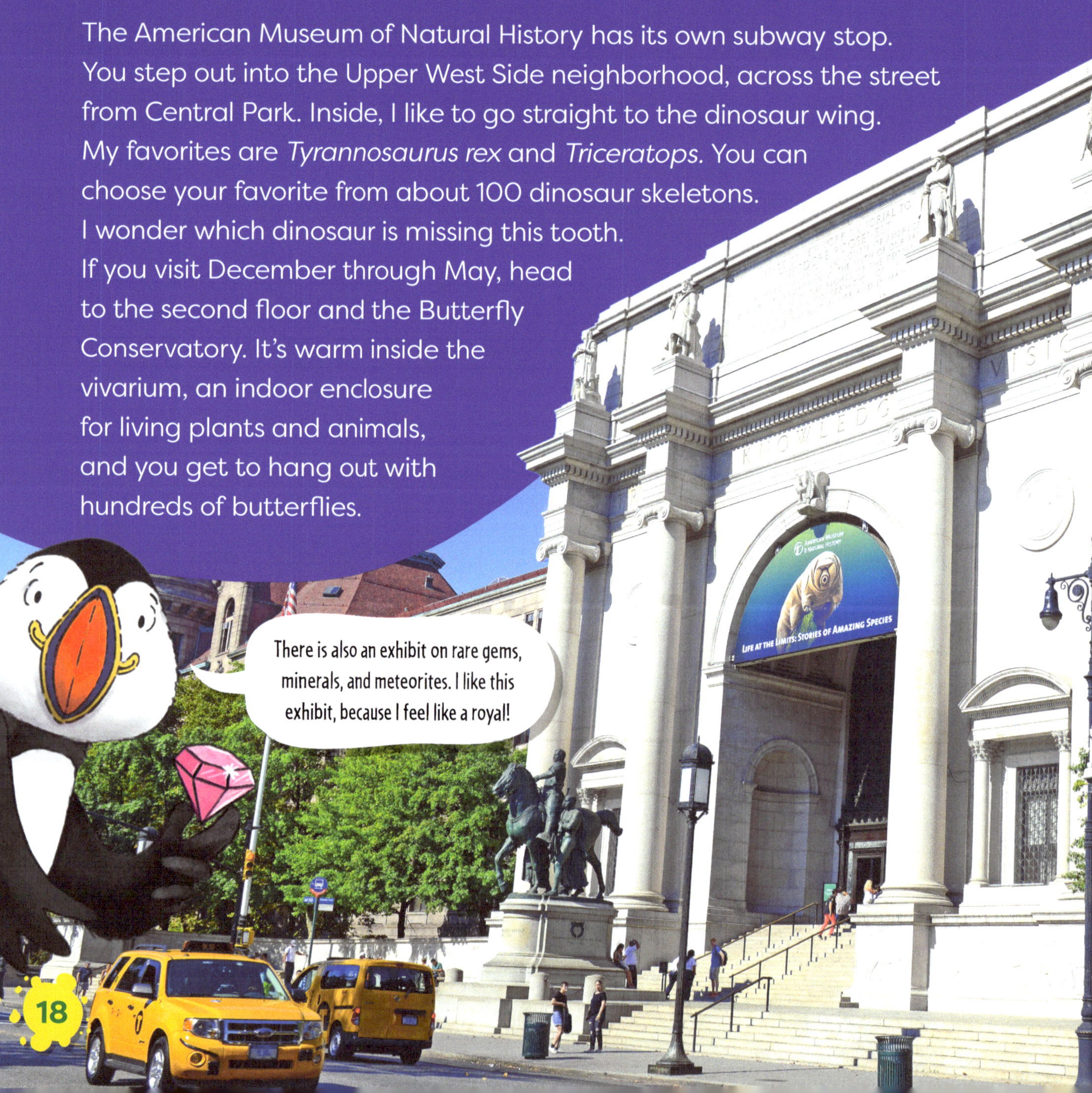

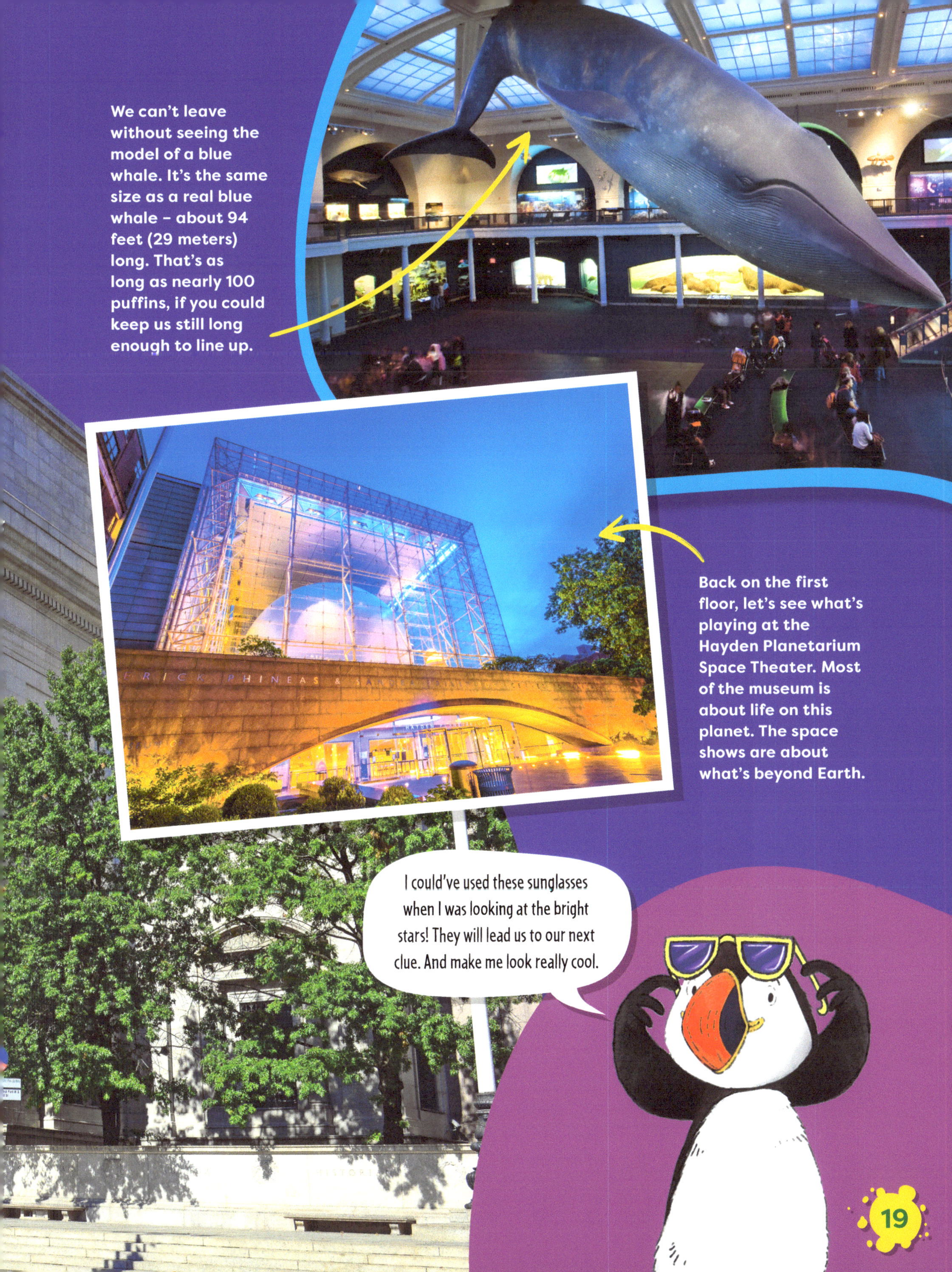
We can't leave without seeing the model of a blue whale. It's the same size as a real blue whale – about 94 feet (29 meters) long. That's as long as nearly 100 puffins, if you could keep us still long enough to line up.
Back on the first floor, let's see what's playing at the Hayden Planetarium Space Theater. Most of the museum is about life on this planet. The space shows are about what's beyond Earth.
I could've used these sunglasses when I was looking at the bright stars! They will lead us to our next clue. And make me look really cool.

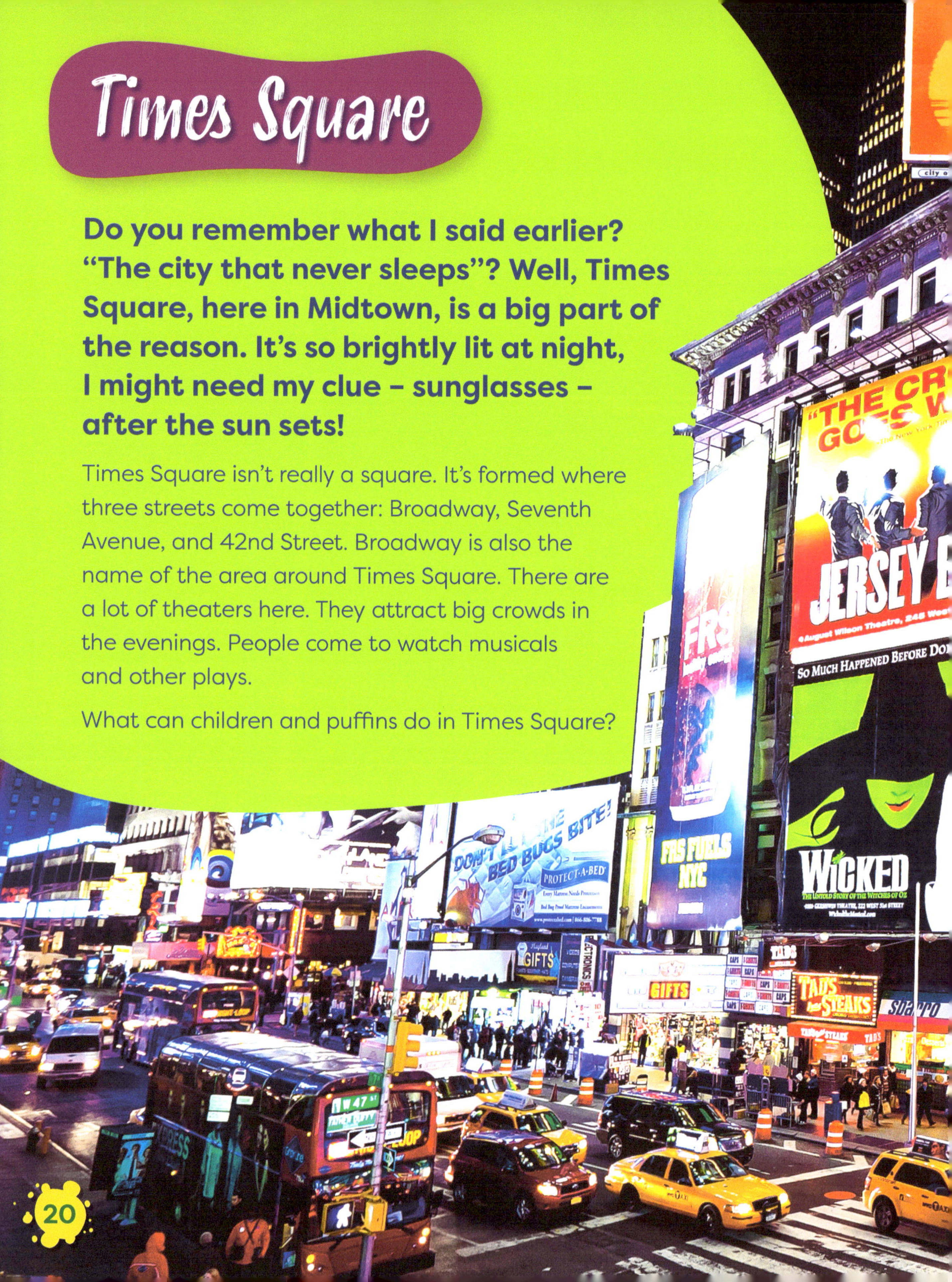

Times Square

Do you remember what I said earlier? "The city that never sleeps"? Well, Times Square, here in Midtown, is a big part of the reason. It's so brightly lit at night, I might need my clue – sunglasses – after the sun sets!

Times Square isn't really a square. It's formed where three streets come together: Broadway, Seventh Avenue, and 42nd Street. Broadway is also the name of the area around Times Square. There are a lot of theaters here. They attract big crowds in the evenings. People come to watch musicals and other plays.

What can children and puffins do in Times Square?

The Red Steps: 27 steps built over the TKTS booth (that's where you can purchase theater tickets). They lead to a platform from which we can look out over the sights of Times Square. Each step is lit from the inside, so the whole staircase glows a bright ruby red. It'll be much easier to see things from 16 feet (5 meters) high!

The New Victory Theater: It's New York City's only theater just for kids.

Madame Tussauds New York: This museum displays famous people, all sculpted from wax.

Grand Central Terminal

The conductor's hat leads us to Grand Central Terminal. As visitors, we zip around the islands on subways and ferries.

Now let's see where commuters, people traveling to and from work, go to catch trains that take them to homes outside Manhattan. Grand Central Terminal is huge! There are 44 separate platforms for trains to arrive and depart. That's more than any other train station in the world. And all of the train tracks are underground, on two levels.

We'll go in at the 42nd Street entrance so I can show you a nifty part of the building. Outside the entrance, near the roof, is a sculpture of three characters from Roman mythology.

Mercury (center): the god of travel, business, and wealth

Hercules (left): the son of Jupiter, who represents strength and hard work

Minerva (right): the goddess of wisdom

There's a lot to see here, and we can even take a tour, if you don't mind the crowds. Let's move into the main terminal and find a good spot to stand still for a bit. Now look straight up. On the ceiling is an enormous painting of a starry sky, complete with constellations, a big word for special groups of stars. We can see the stars easily because they are lit with LED bulbs!

Sports

Do you have a favorite sports team? Kids in New York have a lot of teams to choose from. You can pick one, too!

Two professional teams play at Madison Square Garden, in Midtown Manhattan. The New York Knicks play men's basketball. The New York Rangers play in the National Hockey League.

Do you like tennis? Then you probably know that the US Open Tennis Championship is one of the most important tournaments in the world. It's held every year around Labor Day in Flushing, a neighborhood in Queens.

The Yankees play major league baseball at Yankee Stadium in the South Bronx. The Mets also play major league baseball, but at Citi Field in Queens. The New York Islanders play professional hockey at the UBS Arena on the border of Queens and Nassau County.

New Yorkers root for two professional football teams, the New York Jets and the New York Giants. But they don't play their home games in New York! We'd have to go to MetLife Stadium over in New Jersey.

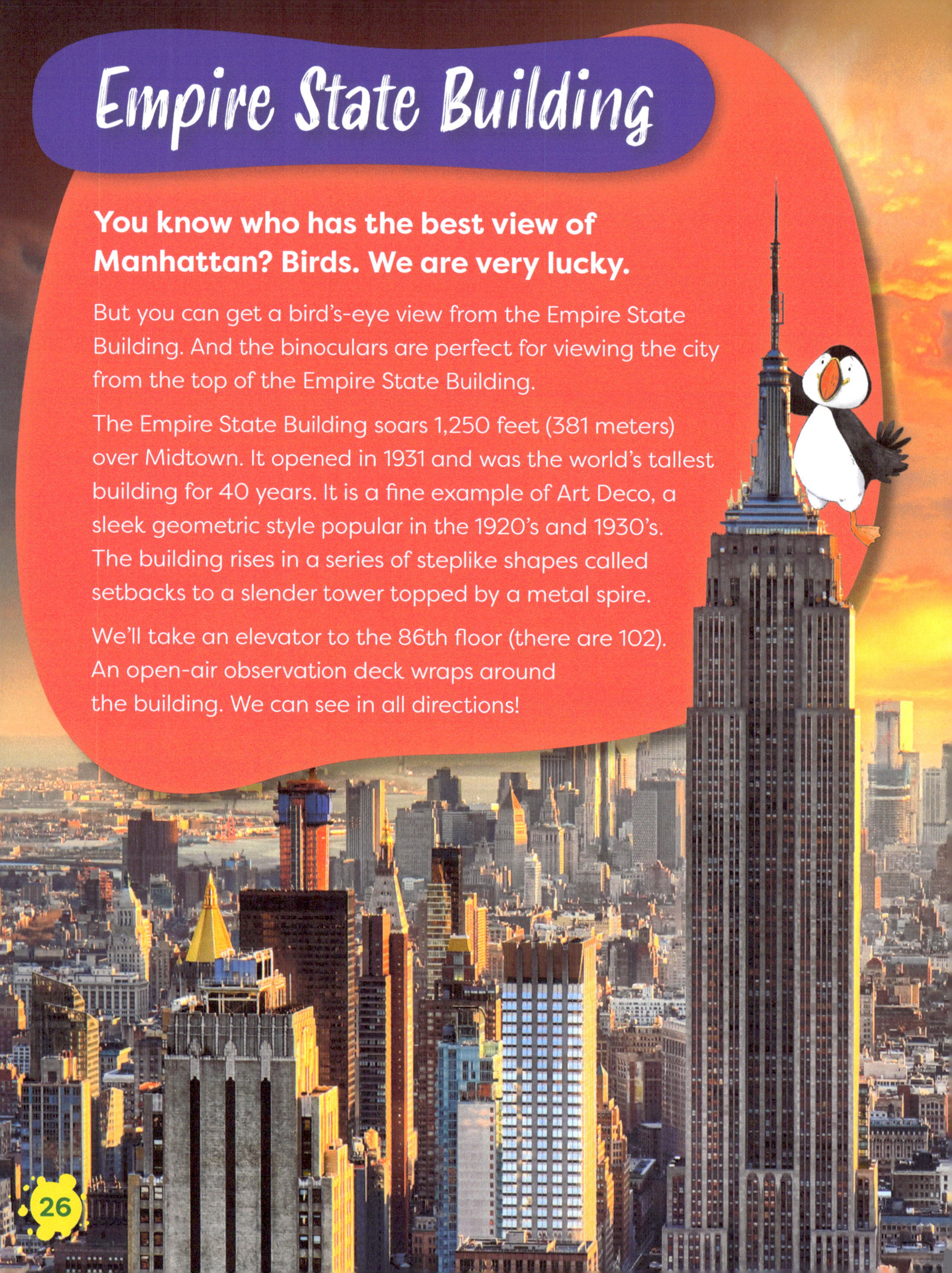

Empire State Building

You know who has the best view of Manhattan? Birds. We are very lucky.

But you can get a bird's-eye view from the Empire State Building. And the binoculars are perfect for viewing the city from the top of the Empire State Building.

The Empire State Building soars 1,250 feet (381 meters) over Midtown. It opened in 1931 and was the world's tallest building for 40 years. It is a fine example of Art Deco, a sleek geometric style popular in the 1920's and 1930's. The building rises in a series of steplike shapes called setbacks to a slender tower topped by a metal spire.

We'll take an elevator to the 86th floor (there are 102). An open-air observation deck wraps around the building. We can see in all directions!

Let's use our binoculars to look at far-away things up close. Looking northeast we see the Chrysler Building. For a while, it was the tallest building in the world – until the Empire State Building was built.

Did you know that, in 2011, researchers analyzed millions of photos and found that the Empire State Building was the most photographed building in the world?

Art Deco was characterized by geometric shapes, smooth lines, and streamlined forms. It featured a look of sleek elegance that was associated with wealth and sophistication.

Uptown and Downtown Parks

This nice-smelling flower brings us to a park I love in Downtown.

This is the High Line, in Downtown Manhattan. This used to be part of an elevated train line. It ran through the city above street level. After the train line stopped running, weeds grew wild on the abandoned part of the tracks. Some people wanted to tear down the tracks. Then someone had an amazing idea: Why not turn it into an elevated park? The High Line is now one of the city's most popular walking paths. It's about 1 ½ miles (2.4 kilometers) long and runs above 10th Avenue.

I'm reminded of one of my other favorite parks: Fort Tryon Park in Uptown. That park is way up, near the northern tip of Manhattan Island. It used to be an army fort. You can wander through 8 miles (13 kilometers) of pedestrian trails, explore two playgrounds, and check out the borough's largest dog run.

Fort Tryon Park even has its own museum. At the Met Cloisters, part of the Metropolitan Museum of Art, you can see parts of buildings as well as paintings from the medieval period in Europe. That means the things we'll see are from the 400's to the 1400's. The collections include paintings, tapestries, metalwork, sculpture, ivories, and stained glass. The Cloisters also features parts of monasteries and churches from France and Spain, and a lovely outdoor garden.

Greenwich Village

Aahh... isn't this nice? Wait a minute. Where are we? Oh, right! Greenwich (GREHN ihch) Village.

Every time I come to this neighborhood, I start to forget that I'm still in big, bustling New York City.

I love these narrow, tree-lined streets. There's nothing else quite like them in this city. Greenwich Village feels like a small town. Maybe that's because it used to be a country village, before the city overtook it. I'd like to show you Washington Square Park, the heart of Greenwich Village. A tall marble monument called a triumphal arch

Tree-lined street in Greenwich Village

honors George Washington, the first president of the United States. Hear all of that music? Lots of street musicians perform here. Some of them are really good. The neighborhood attracts all kinds of artists. Many painters, writers, and musicians got their starts here. Some of them, such as the singer Bob Dylan, are world famous. Visitors sure do like to shop in New York – and Bleecker Street is a favorite place. Grown-ups like the guitar shops and boutiques. We might prefer the ice cream shops and bakeries. Yum!

The Financial District

We can take the subway to the southern tip of the island to visit one of the oldest parts of New York – the Financial District.

The streets are narrow, but the buildings are big, and the business is even bigger. The world's money business is focused right here, on Wall Street! I wonder how far my $5 will go ...

Let's escape the traffic and head over to Stone Street. It is for pedestrians only. Some people I've talked to say it is Manhattan's oldest paved street. It's a little bumpy because it is paved with cobblestones, just like it was 350 years ago. Cobblestones are rounded bricks used for making streets. It's a short stretch filled with restaurants and shops at street level. The old brick buildings rise only a couple of stories above our heads.

SCHOOL OF FILM AND ACTING
Winding our way west, we will come to Bowling Green Park, the oldest park in the city. Do you recognize the famous bronze statue Charging Bull? It stands here as a symbol of confidence in the financial system.
The tangle of streets almost gets confusing, but I see daylight up ahead. This open green space, with the harbor in view, is called the Battery. This park sits at the southern tip of Manhattan Island. We can visit the Battery Urban Farm, catch the ferry to other islands, or just watch the bustle of New York Harbor.
This American flag is a very patriotic clue.

One World Trade Center

We couldn't come to New York City and the Financial District without visiting One World Trade Center. Many people call it Freedom Tower.

At one time, two skyscrapers stood near this place. The twin towers of the World Trade Center were the tallest buildings in New York. On Sept. 11, 2001, both buildings were destroyed by terrorist attacks. Almost 3,000 people died.

Today, a memorial called "Reflecting Absence" includes two reflecting pools that occupy the land where the twin towers once stood.

One World Trade Center is now the tallest building in the United States. Lean back to glimpse the top, 1,776 feet (541 meters) in the sky.

The height of 1,776 feet (541 meters) honors the year the American Colonies declared independence.

One of the two reflecting pools

The One World Observatory takes up three floors at the top of One World Trade Center. On the walls of the Sky Pod elevator, we can watch how the city developed from wilderness to today's busyness. The show covers 500 years in 60 seconds.

We can look in all directions from the observatory. But I can show you an even more exciting view. It's a 14-foot (4.3-meter) glass disc called the Sky Portal. You can walk on it and look straight down - 100 stories!

Across the street is the 9/11 Memorial & Museum, where we can learn more about what happened on Sept. 11, 2001.

One World Observatory

Ellis Island

Ellis Island is an important part of New York City's history, and it explains a lot about the city.

The people of New York City have come from all over the world. In the 1800's and the early 1900's, many Europeans came to New York City. These immigrants saw the Statue of Liberty as they approached New York for the first time. But their first stop was Ellis Island. Between 1892 and 1924, all of these immigrants passed through Ellis Island. Over 12 million people first entered the United States through Ellis Island.

Passing through an island – that sounds strange, doesn't it? You can find out what that was like for immigrant kids and their parents at the Ellis Island Immigration Museum. In the Baggage Room you can compare your backpack to the kinds of suitcases immigrant kids may have carried.

In the Registry Room, also called the Great Hall, imagine standing in line for three to seven hours with hundreds of people. Lots of exhibits show how hard – maybe even kind of scary – it was to answer questions, get a medical check-up, and find your suitcase again.

Liberty Island

Can you guess what stands on Liberty Island? The Statue of Liberty!

Do you have a nickname? The statue does: Lady Liberty. (Her real name is Liberty Enlightening the World.) She has been here since 1886. The French people gave her as a gift to the United States. The sculptor, Frédéric Auguste Bartholdi, wanted his statue to face the ocean, so immigrants would see her welcoming them as they arrived. The Statue of Liberty stands on a pedestal. Should we go up to Lady Liberty's crown? We'll have to climb 162 steps on a spiral stairway – after 215 steps from the lobby to the pedestal! There is no elevator to whisk us to the crown.

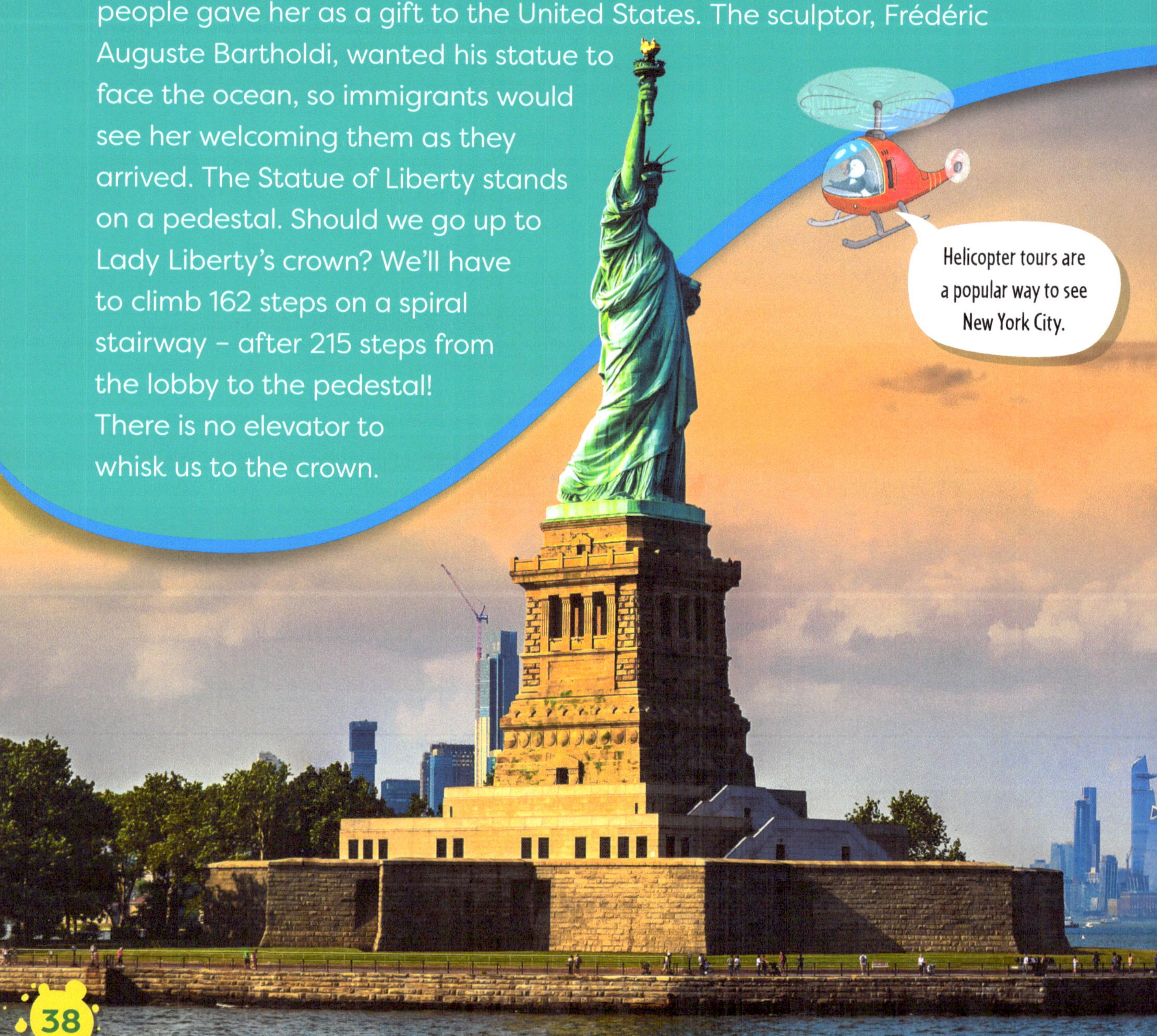

From the bottom of her feet to the tip of her torch, she is 151 feet 1 inch (46 meters) tall. That's like almost nine adult giraffes stacked one on top of the other.

The statue looks like it's covered in green metal, doesn't it? That's actually copper. Over time, copper reacts with air to form a green coating.

Brooklyn

Brooklyn is one of the five boroughs that make up New York City.

It lies at the southwest end of Long Island, across the East River from Manhattan. Brooklyn covers 97 square miles (251 square kilometers). It is the most heavily populated of the five boroughs.

Brooklyn's landmarks include Prospect Park, the Brooklyn Academy of Music, the Brooklyn Botanic Garden, and the Brooklyn Museum. This is why we have the paintbrush. Although I doubt it was an invitation to create something to hang in this famous museum.

The Brooklyn Museum is New York City's second largest. And the museum holds nearly 1.5 million objects.

From 1890 to 1957, Brooklyn was the home of the Brooklyn Dodgers, a major league baseball team. In 2012, the Nets of the National Basketball Association relocated to Brooklyn from New Jersey. They play in Brooklyn's Barclays Center. The New York Islanders of the National Hockey League played many home games at the Barclays Center from 2015 to 2020.

Brooklyn Bridge is a suspension bridge over the East River. It connects the boroughs of Brooklyn and Manhattan in New York City. The main span of the bridge extends 1,595 feet (486 meters). It was the largest suspension bridge in the world when it was completed in 1883.

Coney Island

We have arrived at Coney Island! Yippee, I am so happy to see my friends!

Since the late 1800's, people have been coming to Coney Island to have fun. Thoroughbred horse racetracks became a popular draw during the late 1800's, and the island became home to such amusement park rides as carousels and roller coasters.

By the early 1900's, three large amusement parks – Steeplechase Park, Luna Park, and Dreamland – operated on Coney Island. The last of these old-time parks – Steeplechase Park – closed in 1964. Dreamland had burned down in 1911, and the old Luna Park closed in 1944. A new Luna Park opened in 2010.

Historians have debated the origin of the island's name for many years. According to the most popular theory, early Dutch settlers named it Conyne Eylandt – translated as Coney Island – for the area's large population of wild rabbits, or "coneys."

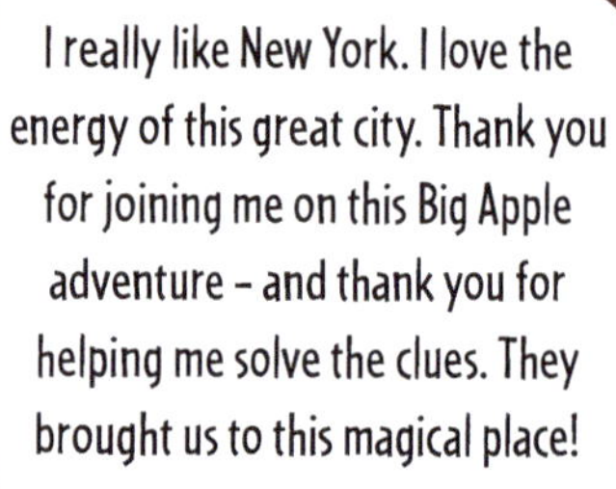

The original Nathan's Famous hot dog stand opened on Coney Island in 1916. Each year on American Independence Day, July 4th, Nathan's hosts a hot dog-eating contest.

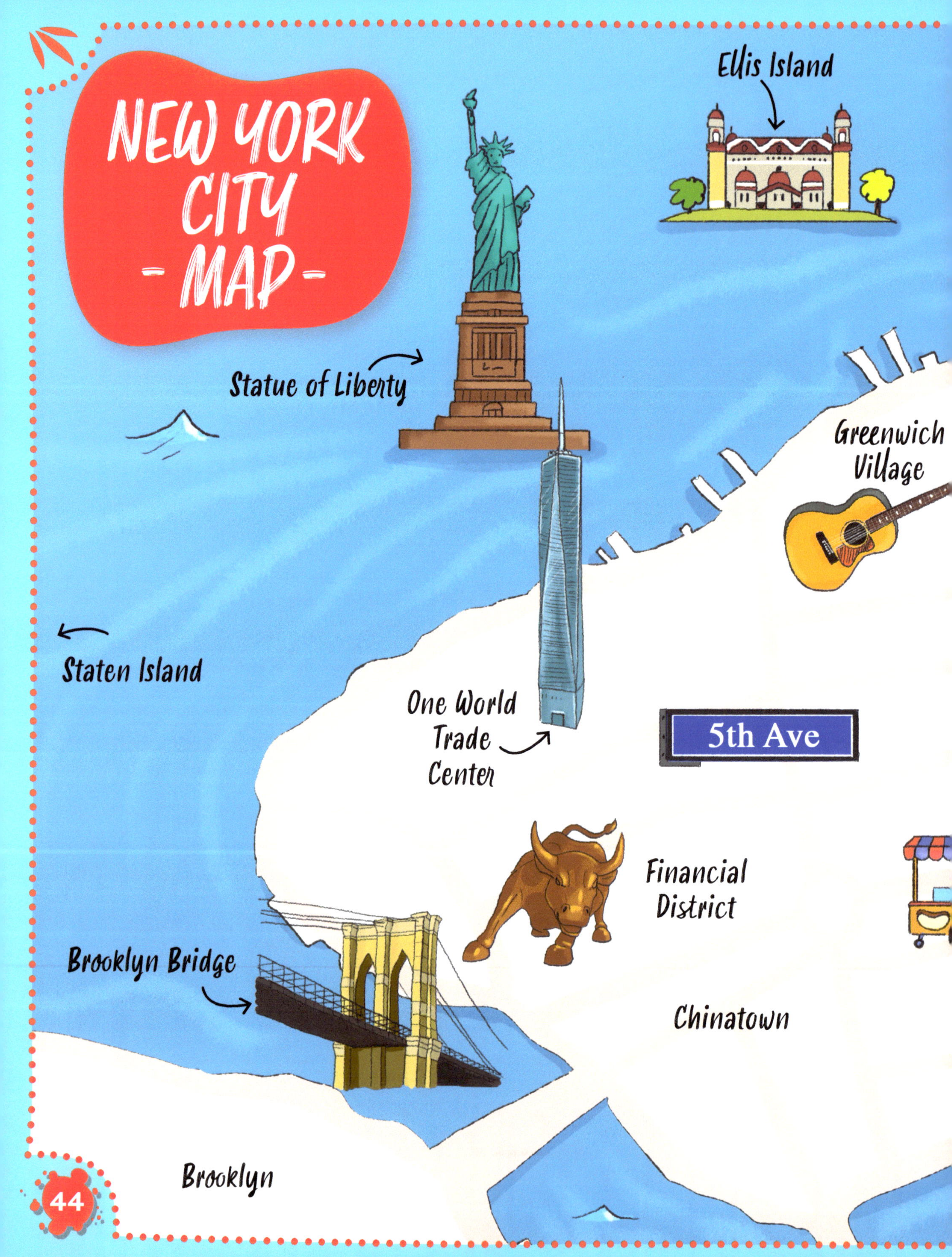
NEW YORK CITY - MAP -
Ellis Island
Statue of Liberty
Greenwich Village
Staten Island
One World Trade Center
5th Ave
Financial District
Brooklyn Bridge
Chinatown
Brooklyn

Harlem
American Museum
of Natural History
Empire State
Building
Central Park
Times
Square
Grand
Central
Terminal
adison
quare
arden
Bronx
and
Queens

A Day in New York City

Up and at 'em! You've got a busy day in NYC! Let's start in Queens at the New York Hall of Science. What will you create in the Design Lab?

Make your way to the borough to the North and visit the Bronx Zoo and Wildlife Conservation Park.

This zoo, 100+ years old, is home to over 10,000 animals and more than 700 species!

Look out for Lady Liberty along the way!

Head to the Whitehall Ferry Terminal, or South Ferry as the locals call it, to take the Staten Island Ferry.

Learn about the diverse past of Staten Island and other New York communities at Historic Richmond Town.

Next stop? Nathan's Famous in Brooklyn. Just make sure you wait to eat until *after* you've ridden the roller coasters at Coney Island!

Cross the famous Brooklyn Bridge into Manhattan where your evening options are endless. You can enjoy Broadway, Rockefeller Center, the Museum of Modern Art, Times Square, the Metropolitan Museum of Art, and much, much more!

You must be exhausted! It's time to say "goodnight" to the city that never sleeps.

Where Am I?

Destination 1

This is the tallest building in the United States at 1,776 feet (541 meters) tall.

Visitors can see amazing views of the city from the One World Observatory and Sky Portal.

Many people visit this destination and the nearby Reflecting Absence memorial to pay tribute to those who died on September 11, 2001.

Destination 2

Visitors can skate, ride bicycles, walk, run, and even boat at this destination.

This outdoor area covers 843 acres (341 hectares) of land. That's over 50 city blocks!

New York City's first zoo is found at the southern part of this massive park.

Destination 3

Visitors can view the iconic statue of Mercury, Hercules, and Minerva at the 42nd street entrance of this destination.

The ceiling has an ornate painting of the night sky and constellations lit by LED bulbs.

This massive train station has 44 platforms, more than anywhere else in the world!

Destination 4

The Hayden Planetarium Space Theater, located here, helps visitors learn about what is beyond Earth.

This destination houses an iconic, life-sized model of a blue whale that is about 94 feet (29 meters) in length.

This museum is known for its fun exhibits all about the history of life on Earth.

Destination 5

This building was designed in the sleek Art Deco style popular in the 1920's and 1930's.

Visitors can enjoy views of Manhattan from the well-known open air observation deck on the 86th floor.

This destination opened in 1931 and was the world's tallest building for 40 years!

Destination 6

Here, visitors can enjoy many restaurants, museums, and theaters, including the Apollo Theater, 100+ years old!

During the 1920's and early 1930's, this destination was home to an artistic renaissance, or rebirth.

This neighborhood is located in Uptown Manhattan and is known as the center of Black culture.

Answers on page 55

Photos from New York City

Chrysler Building

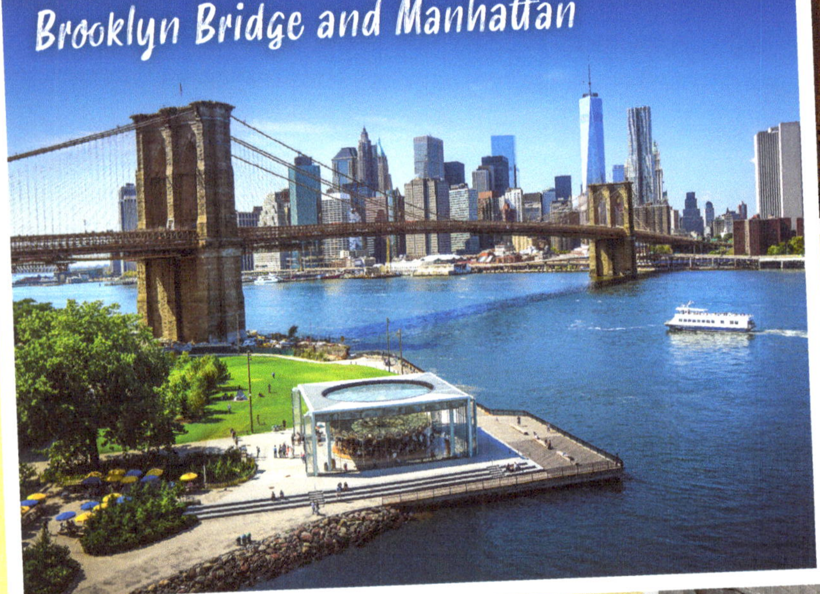
Brooklyn Bridge and Manhattan

Cloisters Museum

Bethesda Fountain, Central Park

Times Square

Ellis Island and the Statue of Liberty

High Line

Engage Your Reader

Activate background knowledge, set the purpose for reading, and monitor comprehension with this tried-and-true reading strategy!

Work with your reader(s) to create a KWL chart. Take some time to discuss what students already KNOW about New York City as well as what they WONDER about the city. You will revisit what they LEARNED after reading the book.

KNOW	WONDER	LEARNED

1. Have readers preview the structure of this text by flipping through the pages. Page 5 describes how clues are included for Norrie's next destinations.
2. Set the tone for reading: *As you read, think about all the different places in New York City and how history, culture, and people have shaped them into what they are today.*
3. After reading each section, revisit the KWL chart. Brainstorm what readers LEARNED from this section and add it to the chart. Your reader can add other wonderings they may have had, too!

Consider these questions to guide the brainstorming process:

- Why is location important to places, history, and culture?
- What patterns do you notice in the placement of things around the city of New York?
- What makes New York City unique?

Use these comprehension questions to help your reader(s) check their understanding as they navigate the text.

p. 6-7 What language did the Indigenous people in this area speak?

Name four islands found in New York City.

p. 8-9 How are the boroughs and neighborhoods in New York City organized?

p. 10-11 Which of these boroughs would you like to visit? Why?

p. 12-13 Why might New York City be considered the "city that never sleeps"?

p. 14-15 What was the Harlem Renaissance?

p. 16-17 How large is Central Park?

p. 18-19 Which exhibit would you be most interested in viewing on a visit to the American Museum of Natural History? Why?

p. 20-21 Why do many people visit Times Square and Broadway?

p. 22-23 What makes Grand Central Terminal unique compared to other train stations throughout the world?

p. 24-25 Which New York City sports teams and arenas interest you? Why?

p. 26-27 How would you describe the Empire State Building?

p. 28-29 How did the High Line come to be?

p. 30-31 Why does Greenwich Village feel different than the rest of the city?

p. 32-33 What does the Financial District's Charging Bull statue represent?

p. 34-35 Describe One World Trade Center and how it relates to September 11, 2001.

p. 36-37 Between 1892 and 1924, more than 12 million people passed through Ellis Island. What does this mean? What did they have to do?

p. 38-39 Why does Lady Liberty face the ocean?

p. 40-41 What famous landmarks can you find in Brooklyn?

p. 42-43 How has Coney Island changed over time?

Extend Through Writing

Norrie just took you on a tour of New York City, United States of America! Based on the places highlighted in this book, where would you like to visit in New York City?

Your written response should include:

- An introduction, including a general statement about New York CIty
- At least three places you would like to visit and at least three reasons why these places interest you
- A conclusion in which you briefly restate your interest in these three famous New York City destinations

Copy this graphic organizer onto another sheet of paper or visit **www.worldbook.com/resources** to download and print a copy. Use it to help you plan your writing.

Introduction:		
Destination 1	Destination 2	Destination 3
Reason 1	Reason 1	Reason 1
Reason 2	Reason 2	Reason 2
Reason 3	Reason 3	Reason 3
Conclusion:		

Answers

Where Am I? answers, p. 48-49:

1. One World Trade Center, 2. Central Park, 3. Grand Central Terminal, 4. American Museum of Natural History, 5. Empire State Building, 6. Harlem

Comprehension question answers, p. 53:

p. 6-7

People indigenous to New York spoke an Algonquian language.

New York City is made of many islands, including Ellis Island, Staten Island, Manhattan, and Liberty Island.

p. 8-9

New York City is divided into five boroughs, which are divided even further into over 100 neighborhoods. Many neighborhoods have an international feel because of the diverse immigrants who settled there.

p. 10-11

Answers may vary.

p. 12-13

New York City may be considered the "city that never sleeps" because of the busy boroughs like Manhattan where the subway runs 24 hours a day and there is always something to do.

p. 14-15

The Harlem Renaissance was a rebirth of art and literature that explored the excellence of Black culture and life. It took place in Harlem during the 1920's and 1930's.

p. 16-17

Central Park covers over 50 city blocks! It contains 843 acres (341 hectares) of land.

p. 18-19

Answers may vary.

p. 20-21

Many people visit Times Square and Broadway to enjoy one of New York City's busiest (and brightest!) destinations. Often, people will catch a musical or see a play here.

p. 22-23

Grand Central Terminal is unique because it has more platforms than any other train station in the world! It also has unique architecture and art, such as the constellations painted on the ceiling.

p. 24-25

Answers may vary.

p. 26-27

The Empire State Building was the tallest building in the world for 40 years after it opened in 1931. It is 1,250 feet (381 meters) tall and was designed in an Art Deco style. It has an iconic metal spire at the top.

p. 28-29

The High Line is an elevated park in Downtown Manhattan. In the past, it was an active railway. After the train stopped running, the tracks were abandoned until someone creatively decided to convert it into a walkable public space.

p. 30-31

Greenwich Village feels different than the rest of the bustling city because it started as a small country village. It still has a small town feel with its narrow, tree-lined streets and Washington Square Park.

p. 32-33

The Financial District's Charging Bull statue represents confidence in the financial system.

p. 34-35

One World Trade Center, or Freedom Tower, is the tallest building in the United States. In 2001, the old World Trade Center's Twin Towers were destroyed by terrorist attacks. Today, people can visit the reflecting pools at the 9/11 Memorial & Museum to pay their respects.

p. 36-37

Between 1892 and 1924, over 12 million immigrants passed through Ellis Island. That meant they had to wait in line, answer questions, and pass a medical check before being allowed into the United States.

p. 38-39

Lady Liberty faces the ocean because her sculptor, Auguste Bartholdi, wanted immigrants to see her and feel welcomed as they arrived in America.

p. 40-41

Brooklyn is home to many famous landmarks including the Brooklyn Bridge, Prospect Park, the Brooklyn Academy of Music, the Brooklyn Botanic Garden, the Brooklyn Museum, and the Barclays Center.

p. 42-43

During the late 1800's, Coney Island was home to a racetrack. Three large amusement parks opened during the early 1900's, but all three closed or burned down by 1964. A new Luna Park opened in 2010. Today, Coney Island is famous for hosting Nathan's July 4th hot dog eating contest.

Glossary

borough *(BUR oh)* One of the five local units that make up New York City

ferry *(FEHR ee)* A boat used to carry people, vehicles, or cargo across narrow bodies of water

immigrant *(IHM uh gruhnt)* A person who comes into a different country to live

New Yorker *(noo YAWK kuhr)* A person who lives in New York City

pedestrian *(puh DEHS tree uhn)* A person who goes on foot; reserved for foot traffic

subway *(SUHB way)* An electric railway running beneath the streets of a city

Index

A

African Americans, 14-15
American Museum of Natural History, 18-19
amusement parks, 4, 42-43
Apollo Theater, 14
Art Deco, 26, 27
Astoria, 11

B

Barclays Center, 41
Bartholdi, Frédéric Auguste, 38
baseball, 25, 41
basketball, 24, 41
Battery, 33
Bedford Street, 31
Big Apple, 4
Bleecker Street, 31
Bontemps, Arna, 15
boroughs, 8-13, 40-41
Bowling Green Park, 33
Broadway, 20
Bronx, 8, 10, 25
Bronx Zoo, 10
Brooklyn, 4, 8, 40-41
Brooklyn Academy of Music, 40
Brooklyn Botanic Garden, 40
Brooklyn Bridge, 41
Brooklyn Museum, 40
Butterfly Conservatory, 18

C

carousel, 10, 42-43
Central Park, 16-17
Central Park Zoo, 17
Charging Bull (statue), 33
Citi Field, 25
cobblestones, 32
Coney Island, 4, 42-43
Cullen, Countee, 15

D

dinosaur skeletons, 18
Dylan, Bob, 31

E

East River, 6, 9, 13, 14, 40, 41
elevated trains, 28
Ellis Island, 6, 7, 36-37
Ellis Island Immigration Museum, 36, 37
Empire State Building, 26-27

F

ferries, 9, 11, 33
Financial District, 32-33
Flushing, 24
food, 15, 31, 43
football, 25
Fort Tryon Park, 29
Freedom Tower. *See* One World Trade Center

G

Grand Central Terminal, 22-23
Greenwich Village, 30-31

H

Harlem, 14-15
Harlem Renaissance, 15
Harlem River, 9, 13
Hayden Planetarium, 19
High Line, 28-29
Historic Richmond Town, 11
hockey, 24, 25, 41
Hudson River, 6, 13, 14
Hughes, Langston, 15
Hurston, Zora Neale, 15

I

immigrants, 6, 7, 8, 11, 36-37, 38
islands, 6-9, 11, 12, 13, 36-39, 42-43

J

Johnson, James Weldon, 15

L

Liberty Island, 7, 38-39
Long Island, 6, 40

M

Madame Tussauds New York, 21
Madison Square Garden, 24
Manhattan, 6, 7, 8, 12-13
McKay, Claude, 15
Met Cloisters, 29
Metropolitan Museum of Art, 29
museums, 18-19, 21, 29, 35, 36, 37, 40

N

Nathan's Famous hot dog stand, 43
Native Americans, 6
neighborhoods, 8-9, 14-15, 18, 24, 30-31
New Victory Theater, 21
New York Bay, 13
New York City, 4-9
New York Hall of Science, 10
9/11 Memorial & Museum, 35

O

One World Observatory, 35
One World Trade Center, 34-35

P

parks, 16-17, 28-29, 33
Prospect Park, 40

Q

Queens, 8, 10, 11, 24, 25

R

Red Steps, 21
"Reflecting Absence" memorial, 34
roller coasters, 420

S

September 11 terrorist attacks, 34
Sky Portal, 35
skyscrapers, 34
soccer, 25
sports, 24-25, 41
Staten Island, 7, 8, 9, 11
Statue of Liberty, 7, 36, 38-39
Stone Street, 32
subways, 9, 12, 14, 18, 22, 32

T

tennis, 24
theaters, 12, 14, 19, 20-21
Times Square, 20-21
Tisch Children's Zoo, 17
Toomer, Jean, 15

U

UBS Arena, 25
US Open Tennis Championship, 24

V

Verrazano-Narrows Bridge, 7

W

Wall Street, 32
Washington, George, 30, 31
Washington Square Park, 30-31
whale model, 19
World Trade Center, 34

Y

Yankee Stadium, 25

Z

zoos, 10, 17

www.ingramcontent.com/pod-product-compliance
Ingram Content Group UK Ltd.
Pitfield, Milton Keynes, MK11 3LW, UK
UKHW060105300726
14090UKWH00003B/378

* 9 7 8 0 7 1 6 6 5 3 2 9 5 *